ostraca

Copyright © 2023 by Lyman Grant

All rights reserved. No part of this book may be reproduced in any form without permission in writing from the publisher, except by a reviewer who may quote brief passages in a review.

Cover art:
a detail of *Diving In* by Scott Wiggerman
Book design: 4doorloungebooks

for orders and information:
4doorloungebooks
33 East Weaver Ave.
Harrisonburg, VA 22801
4doorlounge.com

Library of Congress Control Number:
ISBN: 979-8-9872180-5-1

ostraca

~

lyman grant

Four Door Lounge

Also by Lyman Grant

Poetry:
Symptom and Desire: New and Selected Poems
2018: Found Poems and Weather Reports
Old Men on Tuesday Mornings
Last Work: A Meditation on the Final Paintings of Neal Adams
As Long as We Need
Established Parameters (chapbook, with paintings by Shawn Camp)
The Road Home
Text & Commentary

Works Edited:
Writing Texas 4
Writing Texas 3
New Growth: Contemporary Short Fiction by Texas Writers
The Letters of Roy Bedichek (with William A. Owens)

Textbooks:
Short Fiction: Classic and Contemporary (with Charles Bohner)
CommonSense: A Handbook for Writers (with Lennis Polnac and Tom Cameron)

Magazine:
MAN!

for Colleen
fellow dreamer

Introduction

This book grows from two poetic pleasures, one from long ago and one recent. The earliest, from my college years, was the reading of poems from a paperback version of *The Greek Anthology* and later *The Oxford Book of Greek Verse in Translation*. From them I learned the sweet idea that an "anthology" is a gathering of flowers, and the intriguing idea that there is poetry without there being a complete poem. I loved reading the short, fragmentary remains of larger works, imagining the greater context. More recently, I discovered Terrance Hayes' poetic exercise of "The Golden Shovel." What a lovely tribute, and crafty subversion of poetic tradition!

I have never been one to memorize complete poems, but I have a lot of random lines rooted in my brain that have enriched me, bloomed and fragranced, when much of life seemed fairly dull and routine. So the idea came to write a few golden shovel poems as a way to wander through the garden, the anthology, of my memory, the soil in which my love of poetry grows. In addition, I needed a way to relax, to play, after a previous extended writing project. As they say, one thing led to another until I had about 75 of them.

As I wrote, I began to enjoy them as fragments, as shards, potshards, sherds, and finally as ostraca, bits of pottery with writing on them. The ancient Greeks used shards of broken pottery to vote about possibly exiling a ruler. I don't know what to do with that fragment of history. Maybe I was exiling a previous poetic ego? But potshards were also used for accounting purposes, making notes, and sometimes recording literary works. That's the meaning I am going for.

The poems sat in my computer for several years, and then one day, I decided I wanted to publish them. As I revised and began preparing the manuscript, poems began to reseed, repopulate, and I wrote more. Eventually, I decided that 100 of them was enough. The garden was exceeding its borders.

Here then it all comes together: think of a gardener digging with a (golden) shovel, into a plot of ground and discovering these shards of poetry.

ostraca

ostraca: plural of *ostracon*. a fragment of pottery or limestone containing an inscription; an inscribed potsherd.

[invocation]

neither gaudy magnolia nor
wychy elm nor shady
oak nor grieving cypress,
but merciful dogwood tree

[fence]

leaning a bit, but the weathered wood
remains fierce beneath winter's flakes of old
pastel paints. on paths of crushed marble,
winding and weedless, wanderers stroll from old
sages, roses, foxglove, to gold alyssum. a tile,
glazed and spider scrolled, names each old
perennial. in the hazel tree, titmice forth their old
pipings, offered new for poor, and old

[debut]

for so long the snows conceal the stupendous
celebrations of golden crocus and the horrendous
fetid magic of skunk cabbage hidden undiscovered
rehearsing their fleeting moment among the stars

[epiphany]

no expectation of critics with
gifts to honor the distress
this cold season requires of
us. don't use the word *soul*.
others will fuss and
fret about re-vision, sweating
our tender appeals to the *heart*
(another word poets can
not say these days). bad press

[cradle]

blanket's edge satin-soothes like water, cloth
like a pool, like a river. a fountain from
the wells of memory finger cools the
sleep child sprinkled in moon
light. shadows wrinkle the calm-cloth.
the baby's breathpause from
warp to weft dreamweaves and another
worry-wave washes from a farther planet

[awakened]

is this any way to begin
the day, an alarm screeching and
growling. the consoling arms of sleep cease
their peaceful delusion and
release us. riding in a car, then
shoved roadside and abandoned. again
and again, the hauntings and huntings begin

[dawn]

as the darkness rolls over
toward the west and steals the
final hour of sleep, an olive
haze gray lies upon the grove
below the house. from the
high, still vane, an owl
hears the rustling *could,*
the virgule of *was* and *be,*
the imaged before the seen,
flight preceding the flying.
a child stirs in the vision, and
the vole gasps in its flying

[gathered]

juncos at feeders in
gardens do not seek solitude's
wisdom. the winter sun

[steady]

cloudy skies. remember
the storage shed in our
backyard that will list
when pulling drawers of
seed bins for birds

[this day]

a mistake stalling for the perfect day, when
sun and wind and moisture find the
balance to break you away from hearth, spade
over shoulder. beauty is not easy. it sinks
its blade, whetted and clean, through sod, into
muck's potential, down to gravelly
rock bed spark. cold rain. prepare the ground

[warming]

the false spring sun is a blaze
of hopefulness overwhelming. lift up
the cold capped head and face into
wave-flame's golden,
cresting winter's soot-stained stones

[prep work]

and the chill and the gray,
the brief afterdawn and the skies
hung low on hips, workaday
cloudwool pierced, torn and
thorned, hoed and sworn bleary

[flood]

and so the daffodils' intolerable
joy, the cardinals' scarlet music
disrobing, snowmelt urging for the falls

[speech acts]

worm burrowing as deep as
hedge roots swallowing each rich syllable
of sod. at night the tunnels they crawl from
echo the castings of hollowed sound

[muse]

after sowing, nothing.
loose soil sprinkled moist, so
smooth and flush. small seeds far
from cracking linger, but
the pale plot of slivered moonlight

[shallows]

another day, hands digging the
dirt again. time past, present, life
assuaged in the still-less-nesses of
three rows of peas, significant
now when sun and soil

[trap]

the snare of ambition but
white turns green so slowly,
pea to pod, and so slowly

[inscape]

so always the weather
is, one and manifold, and
like fire confessing, a rose
by any other, what just is,
one way, every, and all
ways, windowwaking you
to lingerlook and see.
whether fasting or drinking
in the stormjoy: always the
tempest inside the dewdrop's
ashfilled soulstilled mystery

[footprints]

squirrels scavenge for
scattered seeds until they
suddenly stop. do they know
depletion's sign or the
signals of their excesses.
the frayed bed of
snow unmade by so many feet

[faith]

could a child have thought it all himself,
desire for light that must part
soil, tidal shifts for coral
and crab, bees' delight in scent and
sight. or were distinct urges sparked in mud
by separate gods for cosmos, crow, and clam

[equinox]

and also rain drilling like nails and hail
paining fading early flowers: the o
of daffodils' mouths winching at greenest
buds. the glistening overhanging branch

[living]

we should know what
answers to expect before our lips
seed questions into wind. my
brain asks what, but my lips
speak how and when and i must have.
in the garden, this morning, kissed
by warming sunshine and
touched by tenuous breeze, where
once a flower brightened and
closed, now greens a fruit. why

[pollen]

windborne, sorrow and generosity scatter and
  touch everything,
like how a clutch of bees imported into orange
  groves balances
the desires of stigma and stamen. a strange
  encounter, an evening out,
my needs and gifts, and yours, someone, or
  something, fitting between perfectly

[taut]

and peace flags pull at their strings,
flapping above the garden in
spring, gayly slapping the
April winds as if earth
told a joke about desire and
let it hang in the air
for the morning dove to make
its mirthless and mournful music
somehow sound sweet

[abracadabra]

always a breeze conjuring oblivion, but
always also already the grime, the dirt under
these nails, right now, summoning these
hands back to these leaves, these petals,
this one rose, charming but troubled, in
this dappled corner. magic awes not in the
making but in healing emptiness.
the lost assistant returns and we regard
the miracle with delight. ah! obey the
call of the small thing. maybe in the light,
maybe not. you want to disappear, contemplate
something great and beyond. return to the
soil and the soiled, these roots, this flower

[wash]

we are all waiting, still
wishing away the fears clinging
like warmed lint to
our prayer's laundry for your
hand smoothing the wrinkled shirt

[connect]

always the conjunction *and,*
and sometimes the adverb *then,* its
story-time companion. paradoxical
perhaps even intoxicating.
but and *or* don't sum to joy

[joy]

for so long the rain, the
rain. then one day sun
dazzles the soaked lawn, and
hell breaks loose under her
gaze. christ, the joy flowers
scream, urges that are
surged through right now and here

[communion]

like the child asking for some
more soup, please, hands patient,
trembled and soiled, peasant
proud and broken before god

[resurrection]

soft as pierced flesh, though
this bloodlush heals such worlds
as ours. whirls of turning, of
rotting, the sorrows of wanwood
riching latent leafmeal.
it's spring, arising. do not lie

[cornbread]

grandmother's Pyrex bowls
laid out. hollows for cornmeal, eggs, and
buttermilk. diced peppers. small bowls,
blue, the color of
afternoon skies, turned pale,
large bowls, yellow, for honeyed batter

[mounds]

open the envelope and poke these
squash seeds into their soil houses.
strange metaphor, if you will,
but *graves* cannot be
proposed for these nurturing hills

[thinned]

you just can't let
every seed beget a
threat or need. man
must intercede, sacrifice
and bleed, himself,
and never yet concede

[happ]

late spring evening, as
darkness thickens the
cooling garden air, firefly
flickers, a moment of joy ignites
a hole in gloom and
glows briefly, then fades

again, a tiny nova ignites,
earth bound. fairy flare and
delight. then hope fades

among the muted green. we
blindly step and dimly follow
the sparks that were, the
waning echoes of wonder flashes

[borders]

forget the chaos that
spills and misbehaves now
unplanned. bellflowers are
lyrical in their wild
enthusiasm, and
towering foxgloves do
inspire. but remember

[sláinte]

sky streaked of blueberry and cream. i
clink the ice of my second drink
renewing that haunted vow lifted to
flower and tree and to our
obscene need to save this ruined
tumble-down dream of a house

[why]

why even ask why.
in the well's throat is
an answer lodged. there
it awaits a shudder of such
force that life's little
gristle will spew forth music
and beauty, wisdom and
joy. no. do not ask why.
the answer to such
questions is ever stillness

[yard work]

the gardener does not confuse growing and
dying. an accountant's books balance or not.
grown children jump into their cars either waving
or weeping. you can arrange the sprinklers, but
sometimes drinking becomes drowning

[treasure]

late-morning not thinking of
much but delicate touch of dill
leaf, a tickle, gliding palm and
light sway of yellow umbels with
scentfresh, prickle. soon summersoft
sun tenders seedwealth in gentle
clutch of fortune's savory hands

[plague]

the stern god would forecast one for
a lesson. someone sinned and every
body paid. now the drama thing
is passé. it's mere flea beetles that
chompchew on everything that lives
and for no good reason. kill them all. is
slug or cutworm so god damned holy

[métier]

somedays, the call and you just have nothing
to give. even the sun's course seems imperfect.
yet young fruit glows idly as if nothing
is needed, at least not what you're withholding

[mcmansion]

sliding glass door reflection displaying
morning backyard fortune. emerald
shimmerings of pool and planted plumage,
yet she's still displeased. her swim suit's shot
of coral flash glancing clashing with
all those yellows wishing to be gold

[vipers]

across their fences, neighbors are hissing
at stingy water rations this summer,
recoiling at gravel and cacti lawns

[be]

say, it would be like
smoke, a breath, an ambiguous fog, a
light and moving thing, like a bee
mid-summer trapped
in evanescent glee for
time immeasurable, its life
daily inside one yellow in
a poly-yellow field the
size of expectation never closing,
it's impossible color the weight of
unknowing, each minute the
density of a dream, its sweet
humming exhausted by intangible flower

[odor]

garden not so much a
body with limbs and heart
but scent alone
where perfume is
rising. rosemary in such
torture where one finds a
shrub rooted in stone

[apothecary]

today no call to weep.
the old rose blooms, and no
misfortuned souls more
need of hope than scent my
fresh cut of this common
rose in their troubled hands

[sample]

in the garden of language, you can eat
any word desiring. careful there, you brush your
fingers over spicy spiny leaves. you breathe, fill
all your airways overflowing, but don't
exhale, yet. the scent imbues you. even your spit
piquants. oh, yes, mouth the savory silent anything,
but pause before parting lips and slipping out
that stolen secret joy. always be on watch

[solstice]

the long dusk nowness of *now*
stretches the hours and they
linger and pause, and *are*
almost never ending: rising
swallows together
all evening in
choreographed calm
of glides and stills. the swells

[spell]

you don't know what hides in
the shed. so in order
to quiet the soul and to
let snakes and angels hear
you approaching, tap that
door, thrice, right-handed. first
wakes, then warns, then magic
welcomes light's quickened line

[metaphor]

are lamb's ear, larkspur, and
coreopsis really poetry
bursting summer consonants or is
our desire for wholeness in

the universe of things
and ideas themselves
merely a lovely trope or
clever scheme. a garden is

a walled thing, but merely
still only a garden, a
collection of rows that mirage
perhaps the lines of

a mother tongue shimmering the
soil. about that spirit

[reach]

bean vine twines to
desire. to do and be.
so high the ascending brief.
secrete where the pod is
growing. tendrils hunt the
hook of some supreme
urgency of morality.
the heartleaf of
shade's thoughtful art

[sherds]

but what is a mind, a life, but dirt, mud in
a field, an orchard, a garden the
plow turns and overturns, a museum
filled and refilled, the strata of manure there
from pallets at home depot. what is
a poem but broken flecks of a
voice chiseled free, a room
with windows propped, opened, a bottle filled
with prayer, a kettle with
its whistle broken, steaming centuries
and centuries of a flood fool's art, old
bits from tongues unbitten, broken pottery.
what beggar digs what field for bidden sherds

[wonder]

and what
stolen perfumed
flower, what immortal
turning appropriates your breath,
sighing

[intervention]

not dour roses, but joy-filled daisies sang
for her. a simple notebook, a pen, long
mild mornings of summer enchantments, and
she rhymed with high voices chiming from low
garden borders, their common tune, until
morning waxed into noon's high heat. the
shining merry of finger ray morning
stayed with her all day. even when the light
dimmed, the cheerful gold centered music came
back to her, winking, grateful, lifting up
her poor sorrowed soul over and over

[scents]

through the bedroom window, new moon's partial light comes
gently, and the odor of spring lilac caresses her innocent back

in the garden, honeysuckle's unanswered dream comes
to her, and the full moon bathes the glory of her naked back

the moon's final crescent fulfills its promise and comes
to share the yard with spicy jasmine before she turns her back

[interiors]

is there any way not to be *in*:
to inscribe the lines defining this
place, to spandraw our swirling world
inclusive, incipient and interred. we
are such hapless accidents. we walk
and are stylused, marked and remarked on
invisibly, geographing internally the
imaginative space of our roamings, the roof
box of heavenfolds lifted by shoves of
intellection and faith, the rockfloor of hell-
fear caved by our morningjoy gazing
beyond beyond. always the prison of *at*
erasing, hand sketching furtherfield's flowers

[pleasure principle]

ghosts grumble inside the skull with
jouissant glee invoked by lively
dances of dread and joy.
the jig of festering regrets and the
waltz of wanton self's abandoned joys
contest, shock, and hide, and we
tortured dreamers cannot
forget what we forever share

[dance]

coreopsis' petal paper
tall stalk parasol

blessed prance of
summer's casual pleasures

lamb's ear's fleshy
dust gray undertones

forlorn thresh of
day's unmourned sorrow

[grace]

often that thing coiled over there with
golden jerusalem's myriad
overflowing and protecting eyes

[withholding]

two weeks, three, and rain
abandoned imagination never
even winking a need
to wet desire, to surprise
softly the crack in us
unprepared

[doldrum]

you'll do it, sometime.
right now it seems too
hard, too late, too hot
to lift yourself from the
couch, face the mirror, eye
to eye, mark the list of
everything that heaven
sees in you that shines

[fortune]

the liquid echo rises in the garden well
and crests to splash the caller's face. it's
dusk. hibiscus petals are closing. father's
returning soon, though he's late this day.
his children unlock the wooden gate and
wait in rising waves of everybody's
hope. the youngest singing true and wounded

[catalog]

soggy sorrow of too much rain
and brittle fear of when it quit,
thick root bog of mud and
mold leaf stain. cracked scabbed. the
soil skin rent in scorching wind,
the rotting fruit the wax wings got
and flew away far and high

[stationed]

cardinals ruffle birdbath splash, like
exploding scarlets, like every
marksman's nightmare. dull patient sparrow
waiting in nature's camo, falling
from birch branch to water now still like
a mirror. watcher, guarding every
morning, fingers roughen table grain,
breathes, eases grip on the trigger of
memory, wounding wind, burning sand

[chapters]

the past's broken arcs are jointed with *once*.
the lines are drawn in ink's illusions of *i*.
memory hinges with the pin of redemption,
but biography's flimsy doors lock to neither
then nor *next*. the cruxes are not sought
but urged by inner demands of *nor*.
once we were unformed; then we always knew

[reflection]

a pool, a frog, an
impulse. an image
flickers of
summer's departure

[admonition]

do not
clutch the
splintered cross

do not
strangle the
chanting hive

[theft]

so difficult to maintain conviction, but
observe your neighbors stopping by the
Marie Pavie you offer the world
on its side of the fence. the polite will
allow themselves to be
paused by its perfume, but never filled
by desperation. they stroll away with
unstained fingers. but the brave break the
branch of cream clusters living
for the thieving bequeathed mysteriously

[watch]

the frightening black arrogance of the crow
the old man's plaid nailed
limply to the cross. both of them
patiently witnessing the ripening together

[circle]

walk around the garden, then come
around again, warier, and back
and again. in time, logic and
faith imagine leaves falling everywhere.
possibility and probability sniff the
other like pets whose entire world
circums on leashes. hopelessness is
a tree, and no branch is bare

[equinox]

not that time's
running out, but light is hiding, like a winged
hawk hushed in brush and tall grasses. think of a
    chariot
parading old-timers, murderous survivors, not
    hurrying
around the track, but knowing the exits are near

[autumn]

the certain hand of summer loosens, then
fruit will fall and eternity's practice
found unprepared. morning chills, the losing
fresh, deepened blush, the northern winds' farther
bend of stem and branch. all, all, a losing
season when fear and fall fail faster

[matinee]

the gray squirrel sat,
tail cascading, on the
fence edge, a lone
chirping singer
chattering wonderful
all afternoon. causing
cataracts of giggled tears

[spilled]

imagining a life without *yet*,
without *except,* without words the
forgiving god offers our cracked crockery,
uselessly beautiful. that other god smashes
the flawed, the incomplete, pawns the
unwanted, worthless, unwicked lamp.
no matter how careful, a child tumbles
the tea tray, trembling. mother stands over

[this]

this single dented searchlight this autumn
evening, still warm, honey-breathed, entices
you, naked, into the garden to confess every
line of poetry you ever learned by heart

[familial]

sage gathered and bound
in twine today. each
bundle a gift to
the house-hold god each
loved-one honors with
hearts fixed. their natural
devotion, honest piety

[hearth]

it doesn't matter where we are. *here*
will do. but when is essential. *now*
is the scent of sandalwood and we
sit beside the nothing-to-forget.
smoke of memory, smoke of dream, each
rises and dissembles from other
embers. the rhythms of being and
breathing conspire and scatter our selves

[dominion]

walking stony, craggy land and careful how
we stepped, we rose more thoughtful than graceful.
the sky became more frightful with the climb
as if god's thin gown brushed close to those
who plod. we hiked until our shadows
grew long behind us, laying self's blanket on
uneven ground, but it refused us still and my
possession, and skies darkened on farther hill

[provide]

from garden shed eave-mud, parent
swallows feed young hunger, darting
into twilight rise and swoop, down
arced to still ponds. broad wings nerved
for cut and dive hovered by
forked-tail spread and what
loud appetite before evening chills

[firepit]

adirondacks circled in friendly
conversations. sparks of laughter
rise like silver comets with
tails of gold. oops. there go his
secrets trailing clouds of wine

[couple]

holding hands for that long walk, and the
 intricate
weavings of cells and spirit nestle songs'
everlasting harmonies between. nothing will
 be lost,
always the music, duet, melody of eternal
 measure

[predawn]

moonflower's lemon breath gentles the garden
    sleepily.
fat skunk waddles from night shadows indifferent

[fate]

why act surprised and
why wonder if.
things die. they
get planted, grow, are
happy or sad,
thrive or wilt about
the edges. you worry how
to help them. they
droop to say you must
water more, less, wither,
too hot, or not, and
in the end, they die

[air]

leave the news on the table now.
fold up all the papers, the worries, the
predictions. feel exactly how humid
the afternoon air is. in someone's life, dusk
is a surprising metaphor. history and the
past are not the same. everything is old,
even the places where there are no wounds

[saints]

faith falters and every
careful saint at end of day
signs cross and bows head the
frightful way they're sworn when sun
forsakes: no certain returns.
so if there's a darker joy to
this fierce and puckish moon, this
dance, this night, this tempting place

[valley]

here autumn
throws clouds
of rust, banked
like bronze, up
the ridge gone
hushed, dark
silence and
shadow deep

[trapped]

don't let them cuff your wrists. don't
go where they order you to go,
down to the station, down
into some quiet room, down the hall into
that dark place to talk about that
basement. don't ask what basement

[discharge]

then they see everything.
the barrel of a rifle blooming
smoke and a child bows
beside classmates laid down
beneath the Autumn Blaze in
front of the school the
moment it starts to rain

[archeology]

first hard freeze and your
garden returns to ruins,
blackened tendrils with
punctured fruit, fall's legible
revision over spring's inscriptions

[arithmetic]

count the hours spent
with spade or trowel in
postures of prayer for various
gods. subtract the hours of toil
they expended this season for
recompense and you

[clearing]

unabsolute order. pulling,
hunched and unsteady, the
dry stalks and vines from garden
beds without pity. I
am certain that always
it does no good to think

[december]

how silver trout swim under thick ice, how
live oak refuse to undress, greatly,
fiercely, how late ruffled summer kale
greens all winter, curled leaves and
heedless determination, how the gentle leek
stalks stand stark, still, in snowdust. all avail
a gritty faith, tightly wrapped, resolved to,
what. not to harm, and not to profit,
not to begin again, always imprisoned in a
desperate cycle of that and then, of man's
illusion that here's not the garden, now his soul

[advent]

the voice inside will say *nownow*
as december winds buffet still the
sparrows in dry stalks. their eyes
catch fall's final fallen and look
everywhere but up

[*blanc* verse]

nothing lasts forever, but
iceberg roses bloom two seasons where
they can. daisies and anemones are
lovely where lily of the
valley cannot grow, and snows
cannot smother memories of
moonflower's scent from yesteryear

[solstice]

so many stories they
tell how about old gods are
dying, new gods are coming,
night spreading its cloak closer,
wider, longer, an ending without
war, no teeth, no beast moving
upon, slouching toward, like
fire, like flood, but snow
falling. swaddled in clouds

[x-mas]

been careless and banged
pots and planters lie about
scattered. winter wind cleavers by
house edge and brooms
tiny gods like leaves in fence piles that
layer the rush and sweep
of other season's obligations. the
cold and timid afternoon light gutters,
while candles for indoor gods burn clean

[midnight]

over the windy porch, alone, it's
harkening, the slice of moon a
sharpened edge, glistened, wicked,
the garden snowed like a white
thigh exposed, un-laced, still, icy,
another ribbon in the fence of night

[cycle]

awakening so slowly, yet
always happily already,
the child rides on
the tides of dawn—the
light sways on window bough,
cold but not uncaring—
into re-rehearsing spring

[resolution]

I practice and practice and practice
and, still, no resurrection

[benediction]

abandon even the idea of *before*.
abandon the thought that a
moment, this or any moment, could be ruined.
abandon the fantasy that this garden
yesterday or today, has begun or begins
to flourish, no matter how stunning, or to
die, no matter what has ceased to bloom.
there is no such moment named *again*

Acknowledgments and Sources

Gratitude to the editors of the following publications for finding a home for a few of the poems in this book: *30x30*, 2019; *Journal of the Bridgewater International Poetry Festival*, 2019; and *Blue Hole*.

Below is a list of lines and sources for the poems in this collection. For easier reference, page numbers of the poems/sherds in this volume are included.

p5. Nor shady cypress tree
    Christina Rossetti
    "Song: When I am dead, my dearest"
p6. Wood. Old marble. Old tile. Old old old
    Gwendolyn Brooks,
    "The Lovers of the Poor"
p7. Stupendous horrendous undiscovered stars
    Terrance Hayes
    "But there was never a black male hysteria"
p8. with distress / Of soul and sweating heart can press
    Simonides, translated by C.W. Bowra
    "The Climb to Virtue"
p9. Cloth from the moon. Cloth from another planet
    Randall Jarrell
    "The Woman at the Washington Zoo"
p10. Begin, and cease, and then again begin
    Matthew Arnold
    "Dover Beach"
p11. Over the olive grove the owl could be seen flying and flying
    Antonio Machado, translated by Alan Trueblood
    "Jottings"
p12. in solitude's sun
    Vassar Miller
    "Summation"
p13. remember our list of birds
    Robert Lowell
    "The Old Flame"

p14. When the spade sinks into gravelly ground
    Seamus Heaney
    "Digging"

p15. Blaze up into golden stones
    James Wright
    "Lying in a Hammock at William Duffy's Farm in Pine Island, Minnesota"

p16. Gray skies, workaday, and bleary
    Heinrich Heine, translated by Hal Draper
    "New Spring, #44"

p17. Intolerable music falls
    William Butler Yeats
    "News from the Delphic Oracle"

p18, As syllable from sound
    Emily Dickinson
    "The brain is wider than the sky"

p19. Nothing so far but moonlight
    Laura Riding
    "Nothing so far"

p20. The life of significant soil
    T.S. Eliot
    "The Dry Salvages"

p21. But slowly slowly
    Thomas Merton
    Cables to the Ace, "#80"

p22. Weather and rose is all you see, drinking the dewdrop's mystery
    Langston Hughes
    "Snail"

p23. For they know the excesses of feet
    Angela Alaimo O'Donnell
    "The Still Pilgrim Recalls the Beatitudes"

p24. Himself part coral and mud clam
    Lorine Niedecker
    "My Life by Water"

p25. Hail, O greenest branch
    Hildegard de Bingen, translated by Nathaniel M. Campbell
    "*O Viridissima Virga*"

p26. What lips my lips have kissed and where and why
    Emily St. Vincent Millay
    "What lips my lips have kissed, and where, and why"
p27. Everything balances out perfectly
    Grzegorz Wroblewski, translated by Piotr Gwiazda
    "Signs"
p28. Strings in the earth and air / Make music sweet
    James Joyce
    Chamber Music, "#1"
p29. but under these petals in the emptiness regard the light, contemplate the flower
    Charles Olson
    "The Kingfishers"
p30. Still clinging to your shirt
    Theodore Roethke
    "My Papa's Waltz"
p31. and its paradoxical intoxicating joy
    Christian Wiman
    "Keynote"
p32. the sun and her flowers are here
    Rupi Kaur
    from *The Sun and Her Flowers*
p33. some patient peasant God
    Mina Loy
    "Brancusi's Patient Bird"
p34. though worlds of wanwood leafmeal lie
    Gerard Manly Hopkins
    "Spring and Fall"
p35. bowls and bowls of pale batter
    Elizabeth Alexander
    "Ladders"
p36. these houses will be hills
    Octavio Paz, translated by Eliot Weinberger
    "Immemorial Landscape"
p37. Let a man sacrifice himself, concede
    Geoffrey Hill
    "An Order of Service"

p38. As the firefly ignites and fades, ignites and fades, we follow the flashes
   Tomas Transtromer, translated by Robin Robertson
   "Fire Graffiti"
p39. That now are wild and do not remember
   Thomas Wyatt
   "They Flee Forever"
p40. I drink to our ruined house
   Anna Akhmatova, translated by Katie Farris
   and Ilya Kaminsky
   "Last Toast"
p41. Why is there such little music and why such stillness
   Osip Mandelstam, translated by Robert Tracy
   Stone, "#24"
p42. And not waving but drowning
   Stevie Smith
   "Not Waving but Drowning"
p43. Of dill, and with soft gentle hands
   Sappho, translated by C. M. Bowra
   "Flowers for the Graces"
p44. For every thing that lives is holy
   William Blake
   "The Marriage of Heaven and Hell"
p45. nothing imperfect, nothing withholding!
   Denise Levertov
   "The Métier of Blossoming"
p46. Displaying emerald plumage shot with gold
   Robert Graves
   "Bird of Paradise"
p47. Hissing summer lawns
   Joni Mitchell
   "The Hissing of Summer Lawns"
p48. Like a bee trapped for life in the closing of the sweet flower
   Mirabai, translated by Robert Bly and Jane Hirshfield
   "Mira the bee"

p49. A heart alone is such a stone
    George Herbert
    "The Altar"
p50. Weep no more, my common hands
    Tino Villanueva
    "*Haciendo apenas la Recoleccion*"
p51. eat your fill, don't spit anything out, watch
    Emily Hancock
    "In the Field Grass, at Sundown"
p52. Now they are rising together in calm swells
    Richard Wilbur
    "Love Calls Us to the Things of This World"
p53. in order to hear that first magic line
    Jaroslav Seifert, translated by Ewald Osers
    "To Be a Poet"
p54. And poetry is in things themselves or is merely a mirage of the spirit
    Nicanor Parra, translated by W.S. Merwin
    "The Vices of the Modern World"
p55. To be brief is the supreme morality of art
    Juan Ramon Jimenez, translated by H.R. Hayes
    an aphorism
p56. but in the museum there is a room filled with centuries-old pottery sherds
    Matthew Siegel
    "At the Metropolitan Museum"
p57. What perfumed immortal breath sighing
    Adelaide Crapsey
    "Blue Hyacinth"
p58. Sang long and low until the morning light came up over
    Brigit Pegeen Kelley
    "Song"
p59. comes back, comes back, comes back
    Natasha Trethewey
    "*Vespertina Cognito*"

p60. In this world we walk on the roof of hell, gazing at flowers
    Issa, translated by Robert Hass
    untitled

p61. With lively joy the joys we cannot share
    Samuel Taylor Coleridge
    "This Lime-tree Bower My Prison"

p62. Paper parasol of pleasures / Fleshy undertones of sorrow
    Sandra Cisneros
    "Little Clown, My Heart"

p63. with myriad eyes
    Plato, translated by unknown
    "Aster"

p64. Rain never need surprise us unprepared
    Virgil, translated by Smith Palmer Bovie
    Georgics, Book 1

p65. Sometime too hot the eye of heaven shines
    William Shakespeare
    "Sonnet 18"

p66. Well, it's Father's Day, and everybody's wounded
    Leonard Cohen
    "First, We Take Manhattan"

p67. Rain quit and the wind got high
    Woody Guthrie
    "Talking Dust Bowl"

p68. Like every sparrow falling, like every grain of sand
    Bob Dylan
    "Every Grain of Sand"

p69. Once I redemption neither sought nor knew
    Phillis Wheatley
    "On Being Brought from Africa to America "

p70. an image of departure
    Louise Glück
    "The Garden"

p71. Not the cross, not the hive
    Robinson Jeffers
    "Rock and Hawk"

p72. but the world / will be filled with the living.
    Mysteriously
    Franz Wright
    "University of One"

p73. Crow nailed them together
    Ted Hughes
    "Crow Blacker than Ever"

p74. come back and everywhere the world is bare
    Ethridge Knight
    "Feeling Fucked Up"

p75. Time's winged chariot hurrying near
    Andrew Marvell
    "To His Coy Mistress"

p76. Then practice losing farther, losing faster
    Elizabeth Bishop
    "One Art"

p77. sat the lone singer wonderful causing tears
    Walt Whitman
    "Out of the Cradle Endlessly Rocking"

p78. yet the crockery smashes, the lamp tumbles over
    Pablo Neruda, translated by Ben Belitt
    "Things Breaking"

p79. Autumn entices every heart
    Boris Pasternak, translated by Eugene M. Kayden
    "August"

p80. Bound each to each with natural piety
    William Wordsworth
    "My Heart Leaps Up"

p81. Here now we forget each other and ourselves
    Wallace Stevens
    "Final Soliloquy of the Interior Paramour"

p82. How graceful climb those shadows on my hill
    Ralph Waldo Emerson
    "Hamatreya"

p83. parent darting down nerved by what chills
    Marianne Moore
    "Bird-Witted"

p84. Friendly laugher with his wine
    Callimachus, translated by R.A. Furness
    "The Poet's Own Epitaph"
p85. intricate songs' lost measure
    H.D.
    "Epitaph"
p86. sleepily indifferent
    William Carlos Williams
    "Summer Moon"
p87. And if they are sad about how they must wither and die
    Rainer Maria Rilke, translated by Stephen Mitchell
    The Sonnets to Orpheus, "II, 14"
p88. Now the humid dusk, the old wounds
    Eavan Boland
    "How We Made a New Art on Old Ground"
p89. Every day the sun returns to this place
    Robert Duncan
    "Circulations of the Song"
p90. autumn clouds banked up, gone dark and deep
    Li Po, translated by David Hinton
    "Listening to a Monk's Ch'in Depths"
p91. Don't go down into that basement
    Cornelius Eady
    "The Gardenia"
p92. Everything blooming bows down in the rain
    Jane Kenyon
    "Heavy Summer Rain"
p93. your ruins with legible inscriptions
    Wistawa Szymborska
    "Archeology"
p94. Spent in various toil for you
    Anonymous, translated by F. A. Furness
    "A Gardner"
p95. Pulling the garden I always think
    Maxine Kumin
    "After the Harvest"

p96. How greatly kale and leak avail to profit a man's soul
    Hesiod, translated by Sri William Marris
    "Works and Days"

p97. Now the eyes look up
    William Everson (Brother Antonius)
    "Advent"

p98. But where are the snows of yesteryear
    Francois Villon, translated Dante Gabriel Rossetti
    "The Ballad of Dead Ladies"

p99. They are coming closer without moving, like snow clouds
    Jeff Schwaner
    "The Stones"

p100. Banged about by brooms that sweep the gutters clean
    Rod McKuen
    Listen to the Warm, "Twenty-Six"

p101. It's a wicked white icy night
    A. R. Ammons
    "18 December"

p102. Yet already on the bough, uncaring spring!
    Ikkyu, translated by Lucien Stryk and Takashi Ikemoto
    "Form in Void"

p103. Practice resurrection
    Wendell Berry
    "Manifesto: The Mad Farmer Liberation Front"

p104. Before a ruined garden begins to bloom again
    Czeslaw Milosz, translated by Brian Glazer and Martin Sabiniewicz
    "Gardener"

About the Author

Lyman Grant lives in the Shenandoah Valley. For four and a half decades, he taught at Austin Community College and served in various administrative roles including Dean of Arts and Humanities. He is the editor of *New Growth: Contemporary Short Fiction from Texas, Short Fiction: Classic and Contemporary,* and *The Letters of Roy Bedichek.* He served as book review editor of *The Texas Humanist* and fiction editor for *Brazos River Review* and published essays and reviews in *Texas Observer, Texas Books in Review, The Langdon Review, Creative Pulse, Dallas Morning News,* and other periodicals and anthologies. With John Lee and Sharon Adams, he founded and edited MAN!, a quarterly magazine devoted to men's issues. His poems have appeared in numerous journals and anthologies and in several volumes of poetry, most recently *Symptom and Desire: New and Selected Poems.* He is married and the father of three sons. He can be found at 4doorlounge.com.